TIPS, TECHNIQUE, PERSONAL RAMBLINGS, CREATIVE NUDGINGS AND STEP-BY-STEP INSTRUCTIONS TO HELP YOU CREATE

Down under

CHRISTI FRIESEN

G'DAY!

Welcome to the fifth book in the series. So far we've dabbled with dragons, fiddled around with frogs, spent time with sloths, tricked out turtles, and fussed with felines. Are you ready to cuddle up to koalas, plan a platypus, get going on a gum tree and engineer echidnas? I thought so . . . me too!

I'll be using as many Aussie words as possible, so turn to the dictionary in the back if you have no idea what I'm talking about. Oh, and to all the Australians reading this, if I use the slang incorrectwise, I'm really sorry!

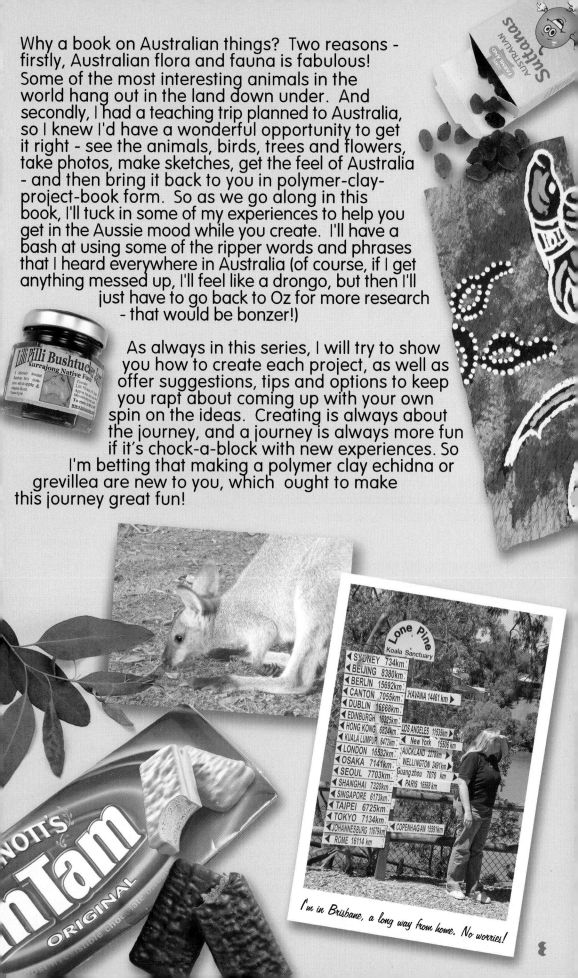

Why a book on Australian things? Two reasons - firstly, Australian flora and fauna is fabulous! Some of the most interesting animals in the world hang out in the land down under. And secondly, I had a teaching trip planned to Australia, so I knew I'd have a wonderful opportunity to get it right - see the animals, birds, trees and flowers, take photos, make sketches, get the feel of Australia - and then bring it back to you in polymer-clay-project-book form. So as we go along in this book, I'll tuck in some of my experiences to help you get in the Aussie mood while you create. I'll have a bash at using some of the ripper words and phrases that I heard everywhere in Australia (of course, if I get anything messed up, I'll feel like a drongo, but then I'll just have to go back to Oz for more research - that would be bonzer!)

As always in this series, I will try to show you how to create each project, as well as offer suggestions, tips and options to keep you rapt about coming up with your own spin on the ideas. Creating is always about the journey, and a journey is always more fun if it's chock-a-block with new experiences. So I'm betting that making a polymer clay echidna or grevillea are new to you, which ought to make this journey great fun!

I'm in Brisbane, a long way from home. No worries!

TOOLS & SUPPLIES

Things you'll need, things you'll want, and some other stuff, too.

TOOLS

Here are some tools that are especially useful for the projects in this book, and for working with polymer clay in general. You can buy your tools, or make them, or just look around for things that would be great to use with polymer clay. If you think something might be a good tool, just press it into a piece of clay and if you like what it does, use it. For example, an old toothbrush pressed into clay makes a neat pattern - good for making sand, and for making koala fur, too! The Resources section in the back of the book will have details on where to find this stuff.

Here are the tools that are must-haves!

SUPPLIES

These supplies will come in handy for different projects in this book - sometimes you'll need them, sometimes you won't - but it's really nice to have these:

- pliers
- wire cutters
- sculpting tools
- dowel tool
- liquid clay

• liquid clay (each of the brands of clay have their own liquid clay available - all of them are equally usable in these projects).
• mica powders (not a must-have, but a really fun part of your clay experience - more of a wanna-have!)
• wire: (this is an absolute must-have!) 28 gauge craft wire is used to attach the beaded embellishments, and thicker wire, like 18, 16 or 14 gauge makes good armatures, and is used to hold open beading channels (we'll get to all that, no worries)
• acrylic paint, brushes, sponges (for adding patinas - any brand of acrylic is fine)
• cardstock - you don't have to have stiff paper to work on, but it's really nice. It keeps your project from sticking to your work surface, and you can pop the finished piece into the oven, still on the paper, to bake.

Polymer Clay

Well, now we're talking! Needless to say, you'd be a silly galah if you tried any of these projects without polymer clay. There are several brands available and all of them are good. Each brand has specific properties that make it especially suited for specific uses - some brands are more tough - like Fimo and Kato PolyClay, which makes them especially good for canework, but more work to condition. Some brands like Cernit and Sculpey are soft, which makes them easy to condition, but can be a bit mushy. I use Premo! brand because it seems just the right amount of mushy and stiff! Perfect for sculpting! Whichever brand you use, you'll have to condition the clay first before using it in these projects - check the back of the book for details on clay conditioning, baking and other important stuff.

Measurements

Since this book is all about Australian things, it's fitting that all the measurements should be in Aussie, too, don't you think? Well, they're going to be anyway. So, instead of inches, we'll use centimeters (although to be fair, many Aussie are fluent in both!) Instead of giving sizes as similar to nickels or dimes, we'll use 2 dollar coins or 10 cent coins or fifty cent coins as the guide. Here's some to for you to refer to!

Embellishments

Because polymer clay cures at such a low temperature, lots of things can be used to embellish your work. This means that you can use anything that can handle being baked at 130°C (that's 275°F if your oven is not in Australia). We'll use beads to embellish the projects in this book, but lots of other things work great too - shells, rocks, crystals, even fibers, ribbons and fabric. If you're not sure, put a sample of what you want to use on a piece of foil or cardstock and pop it in the oven and see what happens. If it doesn't melt - use it!

Some embellishments that work well:
glass of all kinds (which include seed beads, dagger beads, lamp-worked glass, dichroic glass and mirror), natural pearls, Swarovski crystals, stone beads, minerals and fossils, gemstones, anything made of any metal, ceramics, paper, any natural fibers like wool, silk, cotton and fur.

Some embellishments that DON'T work so well:
most resin or plastic beads (melty, melty), amber (most ambers get too dark in the oven, but some don't - if you want to spare a piece to experiment with, you'll be able to determine if that particular amber will be ok), wood, natural seeds, pods (they often dry out and crack), glass pearls (these go through the baking process fine, but often the coloring added to the surface discolors during baking - so stick with real pearls!) and Mintees (a delicious Aussie lolly that is sort of a minty taffy - not good to add to your project, but I definitely recommend using them to enhance your creativity). Mmmmmm.

New Tool Alert! these are my new favorite tools of all time, the "Gotta Have It" tool and the "Can't Live Without It" tool.
see page 47 for more info

KOALA

Yes, koalas are just as cute in person as you'd expect them to be. They are a whole lot heavier than they look, though!! (it's like holding a little sack of cement).

In a way, koalas ARE "Australia" – I mean, what's the first thing you think of when someone says "Australia"? Probably a koala . . . or a kangaroo, or the outback, or…. oh well, Australia has a lot of interesting things! and koalas are one of them.

This koala project is a wall piece, but you can always make it smaller if you'd prefer to use it as a pendant for a necklace. I find it's usually easier to make the bigger version first in order to get the hang of the steps, then make it again smaller.

Which one is the koala and which one is the Christi?

KOALAS get their name from the Aboriginal, meaning "no drink", or so I was told. Koalas very rarely come down from their trees to drink water, getting all their sustenance from the eucalyptus leaves they eat. Apparently, eucalyptus is not a particularly nutritious either, it would be like a human trying to live on lettuce – which would explain why koalas do so much napping!

KOALAS NEXT 4 km

wise cracktighter

double thumbs

Cadbury Furry Friends

Koala

9

They're not bears! So even though a koala looks like a "koala bear", don't say that when any Aussies are around, or they'll think you're a dag. In fact if a koala hears you call him a "bear" he will be so distressed that he will indeed turn into a "drop bear" – a maddened koala that waits for a human to pass under his tree so that he can drop down and wrap around that person's head with his strong grip and sharp claws, causing panic (in the person, not the drop bear). Now some Australians say that the Drop Bear is a separate species, related to the koala, but much larger. It's hard to know for sure, since no one has ever been able to photograph one clearly. However if you're going to be in Australia, and you plan on taking a walk in the bush, you can protect yourself from a Drop Bear attack by smearing your face and neck with Vegemite, a reliable Drop Bear repellent. Just ask any Aussie for some, they're required by Australian law to carry Vegemite at all times, and whenever possible, try to get a tourist to taste it.

I'm not a bear!

START, as always, by conditioning your clays, then mix up the perfect koala color blend. Koalas are usually grey or brown – but there are lots of variations in koala greys and browns! For this project, you can make some good koala colors by first blending equal parts of white and pearl clay. One stick of each is good (a quarter section of a 2 oz. package). Run the clays through your pasta machine to mix them thoroughly. Set some of that blend aside to use for the ears and other white bits. Now, to the rest of the mix, add ecru (about half a stick) and just a little smidgen of burnt umber and silver to taste – depending on whether you want your koala more brown or more grey and whether you want him light or dark. I mixed up a browner version for the mama koala, and a greyer version for the baby (called a joey, in case you were wondering).

One more color you'll need is black for the nose (I mixed black and burnt umber together for a warmer black color.) You only need a little bit of that.

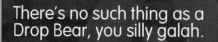

There's no such thing as a Drop Bear, you silly galah.

2

Ok, clay mixes done, let's begin with a ball for the head. Use one of the koala colors you just made to roll out a ball for the head – about the size of a 10 cent coin. Roll out another ball for the body, slightly bigger. Make the body ball a bit more oval and then flatten it very slightly in your hands. Now press one end of the larger ball with your finger to really flatten just that part. Lay the head ball on top of that – this will be the head and body. (duh).

Let's give our koala some nice white fur around the eyes because it looks sweet, and because it's a koala thing. Roll out two small balls of the white clay, and put them in the center of the head. Not too close together. Now flatten them onto the face, so that she has pancake face. (Yes, it's a she – because she'll have a little baby on her back.)

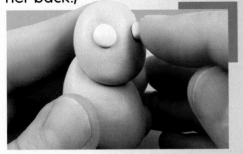

The eyes are dark, round beads – 3 or 4mm. (Many of you that have read the other books in this series know this next bit, so you can skip ahead if you want to!) Oh good, now that all those guys are gone we can talk about some fun stuff... hee hee, just kidding.

I like to use beads for eyes because the shiny-ness really makes the eyes distinct from the clay and gives the critter a bit of a soul, so to speak. In my opinion, if the eyes are right, the piece is right. So, if you can, use dark, round beads for maximum koala personality!

Most beads are smooth, glass-like bits and pressing them into polymer clay works fine while the clay is soft. But once the clay is baked it becomes hard, so you have to do something to keep those beads from poinking out of the clay once it's baked. Nobody wants a koala with beads all poinking every which way! So, what I do is twist a little wire "tail" onto the bead before pressing it into the clay. The baked clay hardens around the wire and holds the bead in place.

Let's do that now, shall we? Yes. Yes we shall. Snip off a bit of 28 gauge wire – about 5cm long. (If you have black wire like this, use it! It really minimizes visible wire distraction after pushing the bead in.) String the eye bead onto the wire. Pull the two ends of the wire up and together so that the bead rests, centered, at the bottom of the wire "u".

Grab the wires about half an inch from the bead with your pliers, and twirl the bead with your fingers to make the wire twist all the way to the base of the bead.

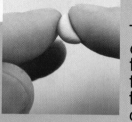

Now snip off the excess wire to leave just a little twisted tail about one cm long. If you really want to make sure the bead is super secure, bend the tip of the wire over into a fishhook shape. Now it's in for good!

Press those beads, wire side first, into the center of the white pancakes. Embed the beads halfway into the clay so that the wires are hidden, if possible. At this point if it looks like a little porridge monster, you're doing it correctly!

The face goes fast from here because just simple shapes make all the important details. The chin is just a little rice-shaped bit, curved on your finger tip to make a little smiley shape – use the white clay.

The nose/cheek combo is just a teardrop shape that will go from the forehead to about two-thirds the way down the face – use the body-colored clay for this. Now just press them in place so that one shape touches the other, chin on the bottom, nose/cheeks above.

Blend the top of the nose clay into the forehead using a tool, or your fingers, so that it is smooth. Here comes the part that makes this koala lose some of the "cartoony" cute look and take on just a bit more realism – stylized realism of course. (I like "stylized realism" because it means you can artsy it up a bit! You keep the realistic parts you like and need for the creation to be convincing, but you don't have to be all anatomically correct all the time.) Use a tool with a pointed tip to make the clay pieces blend together, with just the hint of fur – stylized fur, of course! Start with the eyes, and use a dowel tool to pull the white clay from those pancake shapes up and onto the grey fur of the head. Little short strokes will do. This is when using a creamy clay like Premo is really helpful, as you should be able to blend clay with minimal strokes. If you're using a stiffer clay, just be patient and use gentle, repeated strokes until the clay blends. The idea here is to make it look like the colors are just variations in the koala's fur – the lighter fur around the eyes mixing with the darker fur of the face. I suggest you hold your tool almost horizontally to drag the clay, instead of holding it straight up and scratching it. You want it to look smooth, not like she was combing her face with a rake!

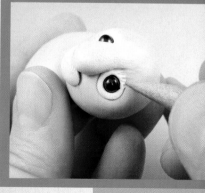

6

You got it? Great! Now keep going. Blend the clay all along the curve of the chin, too. The face should look smooth -- and fuzzy!

Koalas have a very distinctive nose – large and covered with leathery skin. It's easy to fake in polymer clay – just roll out a little oval, flatten slightly and press into place at the end of that teardrop-shaped nose/chin piece. Use the black clay, of course.

She gets nostrils too. Poke the nose clay on the under-side with the tip of a dowel tool to make shallow indentations (they don't need to be deep).

If you ever get up close to a koala, you may notice that the leathery nose looks like it has been tucked in so that the fur on the top overlaps a bit. It's a cool little touch, so let's add that with just a few of those blendy fur strokes with the dowel tool right above the added nose clay. This will also help the nose look like part of the koala, and not just some bit of clay stuck on.

Ears now! Some koalas have medium-sized ears, and some have big ol' fluffy ears – I went with the super-deluxe big-ol-fluffy versions. Whichever size you chose, make the ears by starting with two balls of clay in the body color. Take each ball and pinch it between your finger and thumb to make an indentation. Hold it off center when you pinch to keep the outer ridge untouched and thick. Slice a bit of the smooshed end off on both – this will make the ear press onto the side of the head really easily.

Ok, press it on!

Time to blend in the ear as well as add a bit of white "fluff". Use the same blending trick as you did for the chin and around the eyes – creating a furry texture while blending the clays together. Since most koalas have some color variation in their ears, let's add some white fluff by pressing on little teardrops of the white clay near the head. Blend those in too. To increase the look of fluffiness, add furry strokes with your tool to the outer edges of the ears. Ok, that's enough fluffiness already.

The face is done, now on to her arms. Start with a simple log of clay of the body color mix. Use a needle tool to push the clay into two parts - creating a sort of mitten - a thumb part and a larger finger part.

Use your fingers to smooth the edges of the two sections a little – now it will really look like a mitten.

Use a tool to impress the lines for the fingers. Oh, and by the way, koalas have two thumbs, so the thinner portion of the mitten will get a line down the middle to make those two thumbs. The lines for all the fingers should not just be pressed into the top, but extend around and over the front onto the palm side a little. We won't see the palm side of the finished

piece, but extending the lines around will give the hands believability.

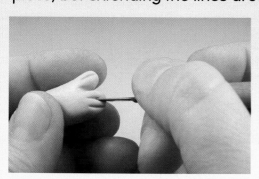

And of course koalas have claws for grabbing branches and holding on to the trees. Simply roll out some tiny little teardrops in a slightly darker color (just take a little of the leftover nose color clay and add it to the body color clay and blend thoroughly.)

Press the claws firmly onto the tip of each finger.

Bend the arm around your finger to create an elbow. At this point, you probably will have more arm length than you need, so just pinch off any excess. Use your fingertips to reform the ripped end into a rounded shape again. Now press the arm firmly onto the shoulder area.

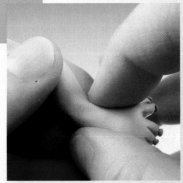

Did you notice we did only one front arm? That's because this gal is going to be hanging on to a eucalyptus tree, and we won't see the other arm, but if you think you might want to see the other one in your version – go for it! (and remember to flip the way the thumbs go so it's a left arm – koalas hate it when they have two right arms. It's so awkward).

Next the back leg, which starts out the same as the arm. For the record, koalas have funky back toes as well. The big toe is a nubby thing and the next two toes are sort of fused together – but if you just make a five toed foot, that'll be ok, since the unusual features are close enough to a regular five-fingered foot to get away with it. Add the claws, the same way you did for the arm.

Up til now, the leg is pretty much the same as the arm. The main difference comes now, with the joint bends. First, she needs an ankle bend. Make this by just bending the clay about one cm (that's less than half an inch) back from the toes. Pinch tightly on that heel end. This should make a nice right angle. For the knee, simply bend what's left into a knee the same way you did the elbow. Pinch off any excess and press it in place at the bottom of the body in the hip area - the two limbs can be close together. She'll look like she's sitting – because she is. And again, only one back leg is needed. She's only half there, really.

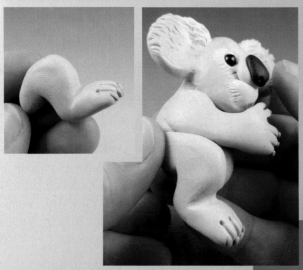

Here are some other koala poses you may prefer

grabbing leaves

A nice finishing touch is a very light dusting of powder. A touch of pink around the eyes and in the ears, and maybe even a whisp on the bottom lip – very light! (I used PearlEx #684 Flamingo Pink and lightened it a little with #650 Micro Pearl). Brush some grey (like PearlEx #662) on the forehead and shoulders and wherever it looks like a little color should be. Use a small, soft-haired brush and just whoosh the powder on. Ok, mommy koala is done.

Of course she needs a baby to be a mommy, so let's add Joey Jr. – all the steps are exactly the same, only a little smaller. You can use the other body color you made to give the two a little difference in appearance. Use the same size eye beads as mommy, since larger eyes make things cuter and younger-looking. (So if you want to look five years younger, just walk around with your eyes open really big. Or perhaps that will just make you look a little nutty. Hmmm, better not risk it.)

it's
too hot
to move

zzz

Once Joey Jr. is completed, just press him into place on mommy's back – arms and legs hugging – awwww, cute.

Well, we can't just leave them lying there, half done - literally! So let's add another Australian icon into the mix – a eucalyptus tree with branches just perfect for lounging in.

13

There are lots of varieties of eucalyptus trees, also called gum trees. Eucalyptus trees have different shaped leaves and a variety of bark colors and textures. The tree in this project is based on a very common variety, one you'd see all over Australia.

Let's mix the clay blends for the tree branches and the leaves. For the leaves you will need two greens, one a little lighter than the other. Start by thoroughly blending green pearl with a little gold, ecru, burnt umber and yellow – mostly green pearl with just little dabs of the other colors. We'll be making a mini-cane with these colors, so you should blend it nice and thoroughly – no streaks left. To make the contrasting light-green blend, divide this first blend in half – but make a big half and a smaller half (all you math-types will say that's not possible, but us art-types know it is.) Set the larger half aside, and to the smaller half add more ecru and mix completely. How much ecru you add is up to you, I suggest that you have a 2:1 green to ecru ratio, or thereabouts. Set those aside for the moment.

Next you'll need a streaky brown mix for the branches, so blend together ecru, gold, copper and burnt umber (I also threw in a little Cernit savanna which is where those little speckles come from). As you run the colors through the pasta machine, rip the sheet up and reposition the pieces to make sure there are lots of streaks of color in the mix. Don't overmix this blend!

To make a trunk with a "Y" of branches (the perfect nook for koala sitting), simply roll out a couple logs of clay. Slice off the end of one of the logs at an angle and press that onto the other log to make the branch coming off the trunk of the tree. Press firmly to make sure it connects well. Pinch - don't cut – the branches down to size if they are too long. (The pinching looks more tree-ish.)

Now let's add wrinkles. Betcha' didn't know eucalyptus trees had wrinkles. To make them, roll out a piece of clay so that it's thicker in the middle and pointed at the ends – it will kinda look like a big, thin piece of rice. Curve that around the lower part of that added branch and press firmly to attach. Add another ricey piece below that one and attach. Now use a tool to smooth the clay edges of the wrinkles onto the clay of the branch.

Awesome so far, but you know that's not enough tree, so let's make another branch!

You can roll out branches to look rough (and therefore more treealistic) by taking a sheet of the branch mix clay, and scrunching it up into a long log-ish shape. Roll it just a little to smooth it, then rip to the size you want.

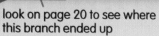

look on page 20 to see where this branch ended up

So now you have some branches and you have some koalas. Let's put them together, add leaves and have a lovely little wall piece. Hmmm. We'll need a piece of background clay to tie it all together, don't you think?

In mixing this background color, it's nice to get some fun variety by mixing the colors in what I like to call a "lookit" blend. (Some of you know about this since I bring it up in every book – but it's a nice technique, so let's do it again! Yay!)

This is of course a variation on the Skinner blend and uses the same principle, just sloppier! The reason I call it a Lookit blend, is because as you mix, you have to take the clay after each pass through the pasta machine and lookit both sides, so that at a certain point along the way you will be able to say "Hey, lookit that cool color" (your phraseology may vary slightly). So here's the quick how-to: Start with several wads of color (they can be conditioned or not – I often don't condition first, since I get more dramatic blends that way). Now run it through the pasta machine at the widest setting. This first run through will be boring. Now rip it all up and reposition it so that all the fun color is in the middle. There's no right or wrong way to do this part. Fold that all up into a nice little package -- keep the most potentially interesting bits front and center every step of the way.

Run it through again. (The pasta machine needs clay that is thicker than the space between the blades in order to smoosh the colors together into new patterns and blends as they go through the rollers.) Repeat the rolling-through, then folding-into-a little bundle steps several times to go from a mix that is blotchy with big unmixed areas to one that is more smooth, with only variations of color and deliciously subtle streaks.

Lookit! A great backround color!

By the way, I used some random colors I had lying around for this blend, as you can probably tell (this is one reason why there is no un-usable "scrap clay" in sculpting – even the weirdo bits can be combined with fresh clays to add some personality to a lookit blend). This blend is mostly white and pearl, with some ecru, turquoise, and Cernit savanna.

Once you have finished making a color you're happy with, roll it out one last time at the thickest, or next-to-thickest setting. With a cutting blade, slice off the edges, if needed, to shape the clay into a suitable background piece. I chose to keep the top and one side edge irregular and uncut, and trim only the other side and bottom. My theory for this is that the irregular edges make it look more free and wild and unstructured, and the cut edges let the viewer know that it is intentional – not just me being sloppy. Sometimes you have to give out those little clues like that or the viewer might get nervous if they are the kind of person who likes things more neat, regular and law-abiding, you know, like engineers or my husband (sorry you guys, but you do have a bit of a reputation....)

Now just use your fingertips to soften that sliced look by gently pressing all along the cut edges.

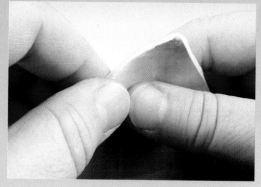

Ok, time to assemble all the bits! Tuck the koalas in the crook of the tree branches, then press the whole thing onto the background piece. (I let my branches hang over the boundary of the background, just 'cuz that's how I roll. Feel free to roll that way too! (No, that's not Aussie slang, just something my daughter says.)

I added another branch because Joey needed it.

Well, obviously it's time for leaves, don't you think? Otherwise the two koalas will have to go get take-away salads from somewhere since these tree limbs are bare.

I think the eucalyptus leaves look really nice created from a very simple cane, so let's do that (but you can also opt for the even simpler non-cane version).

"Chomp. Oh yeah. Gulp. Oh that's good. Snarf. Yum."

To make a simple eucalyptus leaf, use the darker green clay to roll out a little rice-shaped piece. Flatten it with your fingers, pinching especially along the outer edges. Use a needle tool to embed a line down the middle. Twist a little for a touch of realism. Tah dah – simple gum leaves!

To make a really bonzer eucalyptus leaf cane, start by rolling out a round cylinder of the darker clay, about the size of a $2 coin.

Use a cutting blade to slice the cylinder in half, lengthwise.

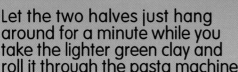

Let the two halves just hang around for a minute while you take the lighter green clay and roll it through the pasta machine (at a thinner setting – about halfway on the knob will do). Ok, the halves have been hanging around long enough – grab one of them and plonk it down onto the thin sheet of light green. Press down firmly to attach. With a cutting blade, trim the excess light green all around the half log, so that it is the same width. Now press the other half onto the other side of the light green sheet, to make a sandwich. (A yummy green sandwich with green filling.)

Next we'll make this sandwich log smaller (also called "reducing" – this will be on the quiz later, so pay attention). Squeeze the log with equal pressure in the middle and all down the log towards each end – back and forth. At the same time press and pinch the cylinder shape into a leaf shape by pinching the outside edges to bring them to a point. This will shape the log so that when you cut little slices off (like slicing a loaf of bread), each slice will look like a leaf in that fatter-in-the-middle-and-pointy-on-the-ends classic leaf shape. The pointy edges should line up with the stripe in the middle – you're pinching at the stripe on both sides. Take your time, you're not going anywhere yet (unless you want to get me another delicious TimTam! mmmmmm). This will make the log quite a bit longer too (the squeezing and pinching, not the TimTam).

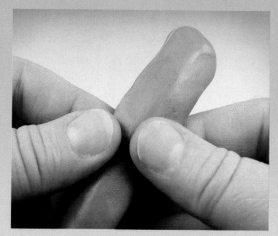

Hint: you can continue squeezing one end of the leaf cane until it is smaller than the other, so that you'll have different size leaves, depending on where on the cane the slice came from.

Now cover the entire cane with gold mica powder – just brush it right on the surface with a wide, soft-haired paintbrush. You can roll it in your palms to press in the powder (then quick! go wash your hands!)

The cane is finished! Now cut the cane into thin slices to make leaves. After you cut a slice, pinch it gently around the edges to get rid of the 'cookie-cutter' feel. Twist the leaf slightly to create a bit more realism – nobody wants limp leaves, so give them some energy! Make lots! You'll need 'em.

The next step is simply to press them on in the appropriate places. Press firmly down on the top of the leaf to attach to the background clay or branches, and overlap the leaves one on top of the other to build up areas of leafy-ness.

As you progress to the top, just stop adding leaves wherever it looks finished to you.

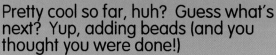

Pretty cool so far, huh? Guess what's next? Yup, adding beads (and you thought you were done!)

Of course you know how to wire up individual beads to add here and there (remember we did that for the eyes) – but you can also wire up a lineup of beads allowing you to add a bunch all at once. This looks especially nice in between branches where the long lines of the design can be emphasized.

Just cut a snip of 28 gauge wire about 5 cm (2 inches) and bend a fishhook shape into one end with pliers. Now add beads – just line 'em up! Pick something that will look nice in the branches and seem like a part of the tree.

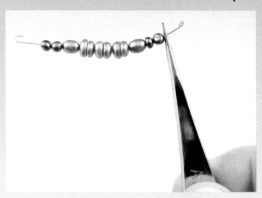

Use needle-nose tweezers (the kind with the long pointy nose and no teeth – just like Uncle Harold) to grip one end of the wire and press it down into the clay in a likely spot (in between branches like this is a good choice!)

Grip the other end with the tweezers, holding the wire right up against the beads so they don't slide forward and get in the way. Now press that end of the wire into the clay, pressing the lineup tight as you embed the wire end – press in with the tweezers so that the tips of the tweezers lead the beads into the clay. Any hole left by the tweezers is usually eliminated by pressing the bead lineup down into the clay a bit. If the ends are still messy, you can add a little log of clay to hide it.

Well, we've gone this far, we might as well add eucalyptus flowers! They're easy, and they'll add some color and visual variety.

Start with a headpin (you can use a wire with the end folded into a fishhook if you prefer). Bend it into an arch, then wrap some of the branch-colored clay around it to cover it. Press the clay around the wire tightly and push forward any excess, so it can be pinched off. Before you pinch, make that end a little bit more blobby by leaving on a thicker layer of clay.

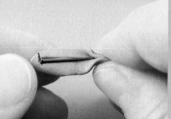

Stick a pointy tool, like a dowel tool, on the tip of that blob and press it in. Roll the dowel tool around to make a wide hole in the blob.

Now stick in a small teardrop shape of flower color. What, no flower color? Well we better make some. Eucalyptus flowers are usually yellow or red. This red is a mix of equal parts red pearl and gold clay, with a little copper thrown in for good measure. This brings the red color down to a more earthy hue. Of course you can mix your flower color a little differently if you want, I don't mind at all.

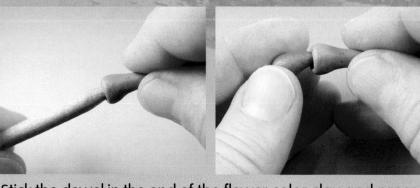

Press the clays together and roll them between your fingers to connect and smooth.

Stick the dowel in the end of the flower color clay and press in a hole again, rolling the tool around to widen the hole as before.

Leave the dowel in place as it will make a great support for the next step.

Eucalyptus flowers are just a cool little fringe all around, like a little grass skirt. To make it, you should use a tool with a sharp tip. (This is one of my very favorite tools, which just happens to make this fringe perfectly. Check the back of the book for more info).

Simply press in lines all around.

The real flowers typically end in tiny dots – usually a contrasting color, which you definitely can make if you want to, but a simple substitute is to dust the tips of the fringe with mica powder.

Make a handful of these flowering branches – vary their lengths and make sure some face the opposite way. You can make a second or third flower on the same branch by making the flower blob part only, and pressing it onto the branch.

Now press the flowering branches into place in the tree by first making a hole with a dowel tool. Before you push in the branch, add a drop of liquid clay in the hole for an extra firm attachment. Once they are all on, look it over, in case you need to add another branch or two to balance the design.

Ok, now bake the finished piece for the full time, in the usual way (check the back of the book for those details!)

Once it's completely cool, you can add a patina by painting and wiping off brown acrylic paint - this will bring out the details and add a wonderful finished look. (Details for this process are in the back of the book also.)

So now what? How do you hang this thing? Just drill it! Don't be scared, it's easy.

GOOD ONYA MATE!

You can use a power drill or a little drill tool like this and twirl, twirl, twirl - a perfect little hanging hole (and another in the other corner). Use pins or small finish nails to hang it on.

You will <u>not</u> need to add a clear coating of varnish or glaze. The piece doesn't need it for protection, and in fact the shine may take away from the organic look.

WHAT ELSE CAN YOU DO WITH KOALAS AND EUCALYPTUS?

FLOWERING EUCALYPTUS HEART PENDANT

Make a heart pendant. Then just press on small eucalyptus leaves and flowers. (Reduce your leaf cane even smaller for these leaves, and then make the flowers half size!)

EUCALYPTUS DANGLE BEAD

This adaptation of a eucalyptus flower makes a fun focal bead for a lariat-style necklace, or a nice dangle on a drapery swag, ceiling fan pull or car mirror.

Press your finger into a ball of brown clay to make it cup-shaped. Roll out short, thick snakes of clay for the flower fringe. Press them firmly all around the inside of the cup. On top of the snakes, press small balls of clay in the same flower color (and in a contrasting color for variety, too).

Pierce a hole through the top of the cup. Bake. (Cushion it on tissue or other soft support). Add ribbon, and tah dah! dangle!

IT'S NOT OUR FAULT WE'RE SIMPLE!

This is another koala cluster - but everything is more simple - simple leaves, simple tree and simple koalas. No extra details in the chin, nose, eyes or ears. See? It still works! So you can do it this way when you're in a claying mood but not all brain cells are functioning (you know those days!)

Fully dimensional sculptural vessel:
KOALA IN THE BUSH

This sculpture starts out as a glass jar (make sure you take the Vegemite out first). Mix up lots of tree color (this one has more ecru in it than the project we just finished). Set your pasta machine dial at about halfway, then run some of the tree color through to make thin sheets of clay that will drape well. Cover the glass vessel by starting on the inside and pressing the clay up and over the lip, over the side, and down under the bottom of the glass jar. Use as many sheets of clay as needed to cover the jar, overlapping the edges. And let it wrinkle! (you can pleat the clay a little to make more wrinkles if you want to). The wrinkles make it look more like layers of trees.

Remember how you wrapped clay around wire to make the flowering branches? (It was only a few pages ago - how could you forget already?) Do lots of them for this tree! And use the same wire center for the larger branches and tree trunks - this will help all your trees stay tall.

The process for the koala is the same as we just did - just squish him right on into some nice little "v" somewhere.

hide the threads

When you bake this, prop up the branches with whatever you need to in order for everything to stay still while curing. I use paper towels, tissues and sometimes small glass jars as props. Once it's done baking - let it completely cool before removing the props.

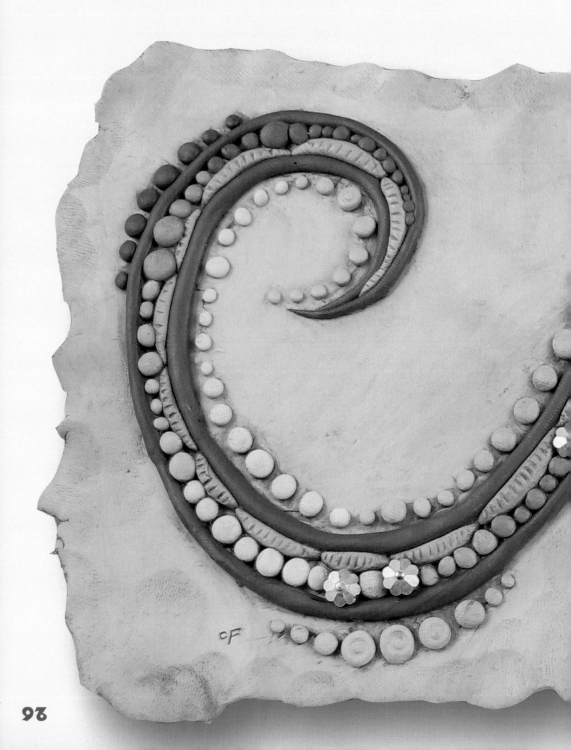

The Aborigines may have peopled Australia over 60,000 years ago, which would mean that they are the longest continuous culture on earth. The paintings and rock pictures that those early humans left behind are possibly the oldest in the world.

The art of the Aborigines ranges from spiritual to record-keeping and personal expression. Many images relate to the Dreaming, or Dream Time, where Aboriginal values and ways of surviving in harmony with the land, were passed down from generation to generation.

Aboriginal art is very stylized, sometimes almost to the point of being abstract. Perhaps the most striking aspect is the use of wonderfully hypnotic lines of dots encircling the images.

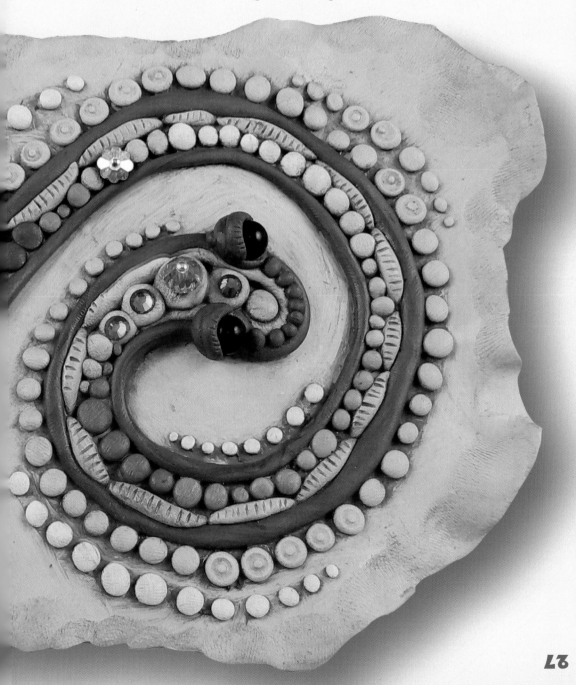

These boomerangs show the use of dots and stylized patterns distinctive of Aborigine art. Plus, when you throw them, they really do come back – how cool is that?!

First step is to decide what subject you want to create and then take a good look at it to see how to recreate it in a stylized way. I highly recommend jumping on a plane and flying down to Australia and checking out a kangaroo or wallaby up close and personal, like I was able to do. Or you can just look at a picture of one. (In person is more fun, though.)

This wallaby was just hanging out at the park, near the picnic tables. I think he was hoping for some TimTams crumbs left behind. In case you were wondering, kangaroos and wallabies look a lot alike! Wallabies are cuter (but don't tell the kangaroos I said so, they'll get all jealous.)

Once you've taken a look at your subject, the next step is to simplify it to the least amount of lines. Try to make the lines capture the personality of the creature as well – like this kangaroo in mid-leap. I find it helpful to draw a picture of the stylized creature, then fill in some colors. The final piece may not be the same, but the drawing will help you to determine which colors might look best and where.

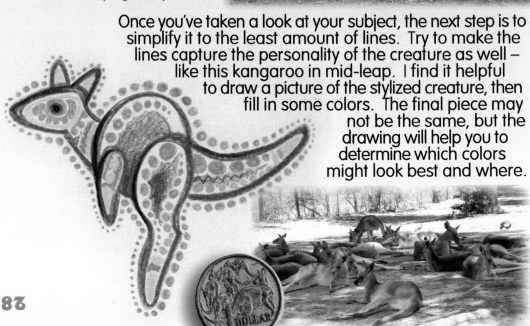

Once you have a color drawing that you like, use a piece of tracing paper to trace over the main lines.

Now it's time to translate this into polymer clay!

Start with mixing up some clay colors, based on your sketch. Here's what I thought would look good. Choose your background color (I picked dark green for no particular reason). Run that color through a pasta machine at the widest or second to widest setting. Make a sheet big enough to allow for your pattern as well as at least 2-3 cm (about an inch or more) beyond that for the other fun stuff we'll add around the image.

Draw your kangaroo pattern (or trace the one on this page, I don't mind) on a piece of tracing paper.

Lay the tracing paper pattern on top of the sheet of clay and then use a soft-pointed tool (like a knitting needle) to gently impress the lines onto the sheet of clay.

You should be able to just make out the faint impressions. Now we'll outline those impressions with clay. Pick a kangaroo color – grey, brown, tan or reddish-brown. Roll out a thin snake of clay – nice and smooth – and start anywhere to cover over the impression, following the lines. If the clay snake isn't long enough, gently pull it off, wad it up, add a little more clay, roll it out and put it on again. If it's too long, just pinch it off when you get to the end. Smooth the joins together with your finger. I find it helps to group the shapes – do the the legs, the tail, the head....

Cover all your impressions with clay snakes. Once you're satisfied with the positioning, press them all firmly onto the clay background

Time for the fun part – adding all the colors! Use your color sketch as a guide, or just wing it! I started with the yellow color and added some to ears and other extremities. Then the green, and so on.

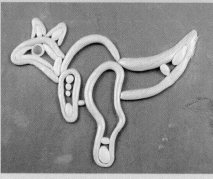

Put the eye on fairly soon – always easier to tell who he is once you have the eye (mirrors of the soul, and all that). For this one, I just wired up a black, round, 3mm bead. Since the clay is shallow, your wire can't be very long at all – barely a nub! Just make sure to fold in a really good fishhook to help with the grip. Press the bead into place (I added a ball of green clay first so the eye would have somewhere to go (plus kangaroos look lovely with green around their eyes).

Keep adding clay dots and bits until you like the look of his face.

Just keep going! Add as many pieces to the body as you want, until it looks wonderful!

Just a bit more… yup! perfect!

The last step in this part is to add some beaded elements – this will bring in some different textures, shapes and a little shine (Roo wants bling!)

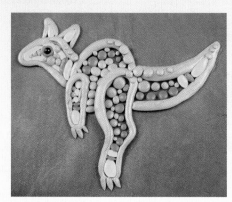

Use beads, wired up in the usual way with short tails, bent into that fishhook shape. Also use fancy headpins – just trim and bend.

In addition to wiring up a bead, you can put the bead on a headpin, and do the bendy fishhook thing.

Oh, and you can also get faceted rhinestone crystals with a heat-glue backing – they're brilliant! Just press them on the clay, and they glue themselves on in the oven (Swarovski makes some called Hot Fix).

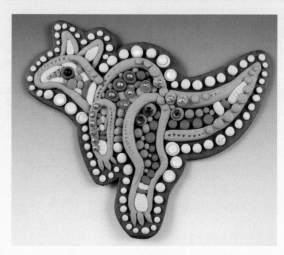

And of course, we have to put a halo of little dots all around the kangaroo – it's very Aboriginal.

Ok, put on all these finishing touches - isn't that bonzer!

Next, use a sharp craft knife to trim all the excess clay away from the design to just leave a thin border of clay all around the outline dots. Take your time.

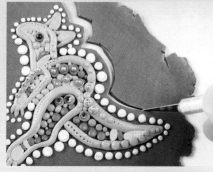

Pick up the trimmed kangaroo and smooth all those cut edges by gently pressing the edges with your fingers, and smoothing the bends with the edge of a tool. Be gentle, you don't want to smoosh any of the details anywhere.

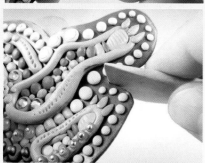

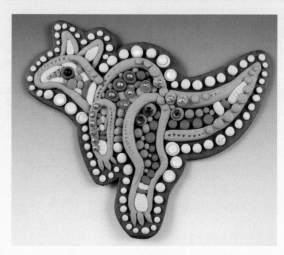

CRIKEY! LOOKING GOOD!

Go bake him for 15 minutes at 130°C (275°F) and then let him cool completely so we can add a pin backing.

To add the pin back, lay kanga upside down (it helps to lay him on top of a tea towel or something similar, so you don't press down on a hard surface and break the clay – remember it's only partially baked at this point, and somewhat fragile). Now squirt a thin layer of liquid clay on the back, towards the top.

Open up a hinged straight pin and lay the flat side down on the liquid clay.

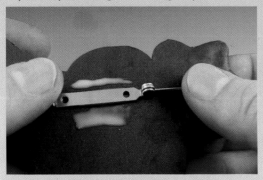

Flatten out an oval of clay really thin –

like this.

no wait, like this

Lay it on top of the pin base and the liquid clay, sandwiching in the pin base. Smooth it on and add additional bits of clay for stability and looks.

That's all there is to it! Lay the piece face down (on top of paper or tissue) in the oven and bake at the same temperature, for the full time (about 30-45 minutes.) Laying it down like this lets it bake flat, otherwise the pin back would cause it to bend in the oven.

Add a patina.

Now, pin him on, and hop on out to show him off to your friends. Pretty flash, huh?!

Wanna make another design?

PLATYPUS

When the first platypus pelt was sent back to England, scientists thought it was a fake! How could one animal be so odd? Platypuses lay eggs, but are incubated in a pouch, and nurse milk from the mother. Baby platypuses are born with teeth, but lose them after they are weaned. Males have a venom gland in their back leg with a sharp spur that they use for territorial fighting. Platypuses have a wide leathery bill like a duck, and a broad tail like a beaver. They swim under water with their eyes, ears and nostrils shut, locating the worms and aquatic animals they eat by detecting electric signals from their prey. Their uniqueness must work for them, though, fossilized platypus remains have been found that are 120 million years old.

Let's follow the same steps as we did for the kangaroo, only this time let's make the platypus into a pendant for a really flash necklace.

Sketch your design, and then copy the outlines onto tracing paper. Use a tool to impress the outlines onto the surface of clay. (I used blue clay, since platypuses are aquatic, obviously!)

Begin to cover over the outlines with those fun little snakes of clay. (By the way, use white, silver and burnt umber mixed together to make the right color for platypus fur.)

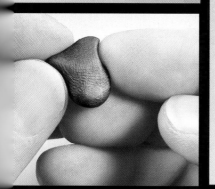

Make the bill out of black clay (or better yet, black mixed with some ultramarine blue to make it a richer color). Shape a small, flat oval and the pinch the upper corners into points. Flatten the top, and tah dah! – instant platypus bill!

Once your outline is complete, add the eyes! (These are drop beads, smooshed in at a slight angle – platypus eyes are a little elongated-looking because of the way their fur goes.)

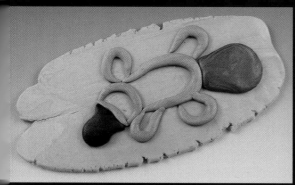

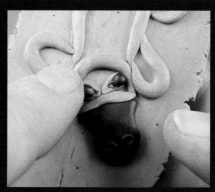

I got a little fancy on the tail, using lineups of beads to accentuate the length. These are done in the usual way – fishhook bent in the end of the wire, line up the beads, trim the excess and bend a hook in the other end. Use needle nose tweezers for easier placement.

Now add dots, lines and beads! Yay!!! (I added some Swarovski crystal flower-shaped beads. Sparkley!) Stick them on a headpin, trim the excess and bend the point before adding them.

Give it a quick bake to set, just like we did for the kangaroo pin. Let it cool completely.

To add a stringing channel, so this can be strung on a necklace, let's first add an additional layer of clay – for strength and just because it looks cool. Roll the clay through the pasta machine at the second or third thickest setting. Now lay the baked platypus on top of this clay and trace an outline all around the piece – about half a cm or so (about a quarter of an inch) away from the piece.

Take the platypus off and set him aside to eat worms while he waits. Don't worry, that's a good thing for a platypus. With a sharp craft knife, cut out the shape all along the outline. Pick up the cutout and smooth it with your fingers so the cut edge is nice and smooth.

Now snip a piece of thick wire – 16 or 18 gauge – and lay it on top of the clay. Press it into the clay – about halfway through the clay – not too much or it will slice right through it. That would be sad.

Cover the wire with a flattened snake of clay and smooth that on with a tool.

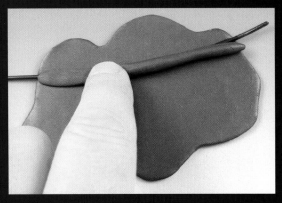

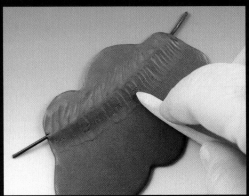

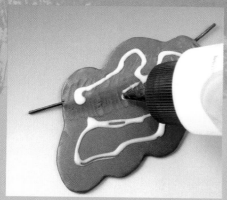

Now slather on some liquid clay so the baked piece will grab on. Stick the baked platypus on! Press firmly and wiggle a little so the liquid clay really grabs.

Add a nice layer of dots connecting the background piece to the platypus piece.

Bake it! – the usual time and temperature. Cool completely, and then add a patina if you want to (remember that the information on how to do this is in the back of the book). Add a clear coating (info in the back on this, also).

And string it up! Clip it around your neck and go show it off, you look just ducky!

Isn't this Italian mesh ribbon cool? and the lava rock beads?! Check the Resources in the back to find out where to find cool stuff to use in your sculpting.

Ok, are you having fun with this Aborigine-inspired styling? Me too! Here's a plethora of Aussie animals that would make great projects! (Yes, plethora is a word, although it sounds like it would be a great name for a creature – the Yellow-Banded Plethora – why don't you make one of those, too).

A **Brush Turkey** tail fans out sideways, but they don't notice because they're always too busy kicking ground debris all around. They are pretty proud of their fancy face coloring, too (although, just between you and me, it's a bit much).

Wombats are playful and intelligent. There are many different species throughout Australia. The wombat is one of he largest burrowing animals in the world, spending up to two-thirds of its life underground. Their burrows can meander up to 30 metres long, connecting with other wombat burrows to form a network that is used for generations. An underground wombat wonderland!

Goannas can grow up to 2 metres long, and are found throughout Australia. They can be aggressive, making a loud hissing sound.

Add a thick snake of clay to give these drop beads enough clay to be pressed into. They add a nice dimensional aspect (even though real goannas don't have a back ridge – but I won't tell if you don't.

The **Emu** is the second tallest bird in the world (the ostrich is taller) and the second fastest (the ostrich is faster.Darn that ostrich!)

Little notches all around the edge are a nice finishing trick.

More Swarovski HeatFix flat back rhinestone crystals. You gotta' love 'em!

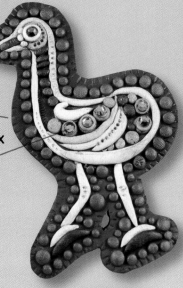

The **Bilby** is an endangered animal, and very few are left in the wild. In an effort to preserve the species, this animal has now become the counterpart to the easter bunny, with "Easter Bilby" stuffed animals and chocolates helping raise awareness of this wonderfully cute creature.

BILBY

Use the ball end of an embossing tool to press in these little balls of clay. It makes a sweet little dimple.

Sulphur Crested Cockatoo

The **Galah** is a type of cockatoo with beautiful pale pink and grey plumage. They travel in large, noisy flocks, and have a fun bouncy way of flying. Sometimes they hang upside down (silly galahs!)

During mating season, a male **Palm Cockatoo** will choose a stick and trim it with his beak to just the right size. Then he will use it on a hollow branch to perform a drum solo. Apparently the females are pretty impressed with that. Hmmm, but then both male and female Palm Cockatoos have been known to drum enthusiastically when the chicks finally leave the nest, so maybe it's just a celebration kind of thing.

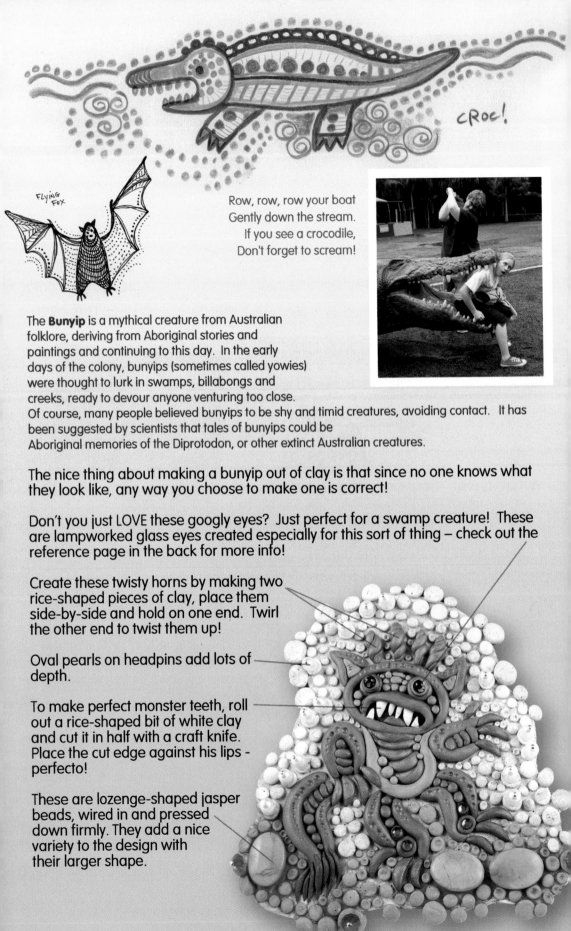

CROC!

FLYING FOX

Row, row, row your boat
Gently down the stream.
If you see a crocodile,
Don't forget to scream!

The **Bunyip** is a mythical creature from Australian folklore, deriving from Aboriginal stories and paintings and continuing to this day. In the early days of the colony, bunyips (sometimes called yowies) were thought to lurk in swamps, billabongs and creeks, ready to devour anyone venturing too close.
Of course, many people believed bunyips to be shy and timid creatures, avoiding contact. It has been suggested by scientists that tales of bunyips could be Aboriginal memories of the Diprotodon, or other extinct Australian creatures.

The nice thing about making a bunyip out of clay is that since no one knows what they look like, any way you choose to make one is correct!

Don't you just LOVE these googly eyes? Just perfect for a swamp creature! These are lampworked glass eyes created especially for this sort of thing – check out the reference page in the back for more info!

Create these twisty horns by making two rice-shaped pieces of clay, place them side-by-side and hold on one end. Twirl the other end to twist them up!

Oval pearls on headpins add lots of depth.

To make perfect monster teeth, roll out a rice-shaped bit of white clay and cut it in half with a craft knife. Place the cut edge against his lips - perfecto!

These are lozenge-shaped jasper beads, wired in and pressed down firmly. They add a nice variety to the design with their larger shape.

KOOKABURRA

The **Kookaburra** has a loud, maniacal, laughing call. Unfortunately, they like to let it rip at the crack of dawn, and right outside the bedroom window. But how can you be angry at that cute face?

I can! Kookaburras eat lizards like me, and that's just rude.

Betcha' didn't know that a **Tasmanian Devil** has whiskers on its face and front legs that allow it to feel its way along in the dark. Up until about 600 years ago, Tasmanian Devils still existed on the Australian mainland. They do not spin around in circles hardly at all.

SUGAR GLIDER

TAZMANIAN DEVIL

The **Numbat** is one of the only marsupials active during the day. It eats only termites, which it locatesby scent. Smelly ol' termites.

Make little scratchy lines with your needle tool for fur, then fill in his belly with brown paint when you patina.

G'day! I'm taking a wander over to page 42 to visit my cousin Bruce.

grevillea

Italian wire mesh ribbon -- use glue or liquid clay on cut ends so they won't unravel

curl

roll out a snake, add little bits of clay...

... and roll it up!

i dunno what this one is. something funky.

tree fern

kangaroo paw flower

fresh water pearl

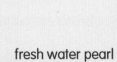

press in notches

protea

pokeyplant

telopea

leaves

make a protea pendant

1 make pendant base add leaf and first circle of petals

2 add second circle of petals

3 make cone-shaped base and add snakes of clay

4 slice in order to add to petals

5 first add drop of liquid clay, then place cone on top.

push petals in toward cone

6 petals positioned. add leaves and embellish with dots and texture

finished protea pendant

G'day
Bruce!

ECHIDNA

There are so many Australian things we could create – so why end this book with a little echidna sculpture? Oh, just because. Actually, I really like echidnas – they are a wonderful combination of cute and weird, which I have to admit really appeals to me (hmmm, what does that say about me, I wonder?) Making one is easy and fun. Plus, once you're finished, and your echidna is looking up at you from your desktop, or skittering across the top of your computer, or hiding in the potpourri in the bathroom, you'll wonder how you ever got along without your pokey little pal.

First mix an echidna color. A grayish-tan color is just the thing – blend together ecru, silver and a bit of burnt umber clays. Add a bit of white to lighten the color, if you wish.

Begin by rolling out a ball of this color, about the size of a 50 cent coin. Make sure it's nice and smooth all around.

Echidnas have a long snout with nostrils on the top – cute in a goofy sorta' way. To make this shape, use your fingers to pull and pinch one side of the ball into a taper. Turn the clay around and around as you pinch, making the shape smooth. Don't try to

get the tapered point all in one go, ease it out, pinching gently and pulling from all sides until you have a nice smooth transition from roundy body to pointy snout.

Make the tip of the snout into his nose by pressing it with your fingertip so that it ends in a slight bulge – just a little! Now give it a

gentle upturn – just pull it up a little. Yeah, like that.

He needs a little ridge to separate nose from snout – it's an echidna thing. Use a tool to embed a soft line into the clay.

Echidna's noses are very sensitive (what with sniffing out ants and termites all the time), so he definitely needs those nostrils. Just two pokes with the tip of a softly pointed tool will do it. Not something really pointy like a needle tool, more like a dowel tool or knitting needle. The nostrils are right up on the top.

Now he smells.

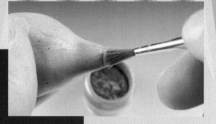

Let's powder his nose! It will look so cute with just a little dusting of pinkishness on the end. (I used PearlEx SuperRusset #654 mixed with a little Flamingo Pink #684 for a more earthy pinkishness.)

The eyes are next. Wire up a pair of dark, round beads (I suggest 3mm black onyx or glass). You don't want his eyes to be too big (or he'll look like an alien more than an echidna). Embed them into the base of the snout – not too far back into the body, but right where the snout starts to taper into the body. Make sure the beads are pressed firmly into the clay, so that they are halfway buried, otherwise he'll look like he's going to pop his eyes right out of his head. That's not a good look for an echidna (the other echidnas will laugh at him.)

Don't forget to check that the eyes are evenly placed before pressing them in. You don't want a crazy face echidna, do you?

Echindas are short little fellows, very well adapted for digging (watch out when they get going!), so they have stumpy little legs, and thick, strong claws. To make the legs, simply roll out little balls of clay from the same body color, then form the ball into a short teardrop. Press the teardrops onto the underside of the body – one at each "corner" (on a round shape? Well that just makes no sense... aw, you know what I mean).
Pointy end towards the center and rounded end sticking out. Blend the pointy end into the belly to attach the legs.

Claws are simple, but first let's mix up a claw color. We could have done this at the beginning, but I forgot. Take some of the body color (just a little blob – about the size of the leg balls you just made) and thoroughly blend it with an equal amount of burnt umber clay to make a ripper claw color. Ok, now the claws are rice-sized and rice-shaped bits. You'll need four per leg.

Stick 'em on! Just press them firmly onto the underside of the legs.

Echidnas, like many Australian animals, are a wonderfully unusual! It's young are born as eggs, incubated in a pouch (they're marsupials of course!) and they nurse from the mother. Echidnas eat ants and termites. Yummy. Sometimes an echidna will lie on an ant mound with its tongue lying out for the ants to crawl over. Then, Slurp! Chomp! Gulp! Echidnas roll into a ball when threatened, presenting a ball of spikes to the intruder. An echidna can lift objects up to twice its own weight, yet not one has ever won the IronMan contest.

For a finishing touch, smooth the joints between the leg and body by just pressing and pulling the clay with a tool. You don't have to do this step, but it looks good if you do.

The short spikes that make the echidna so delightfully pokey grow up out of a dense mat of shorter hairy fur. Let's scribble the surface of his back to make that under-hair. Use the tip of a dowel tool, or even a needle tool (I like the dowel tool best for this). In order to prevent squashing his legs, I suggest that you hold him with support under the belly so that you can scribble all over! Up to the eyes, down over the legs, right down to the under-side – scribble, scribble, scrbble!

He should look like this now - a hairy potato creature!

I recommend that we give the little guy a short bake in the oven before we add the spikes. This is a good thing to do because it firms up all the details and allows you to press on all the spikes without mushing anything you've done so far. Go bake him for about 20 minutes.

Now, the next part is a little tedious, but easy – you just have to put seventy thousand spikes on his back. Ok, maybe not that many – sixty thousand.

The spikes need to be a little lighter than the echidna's body, so just take some of the leftover body color and mix it with white and ecru – about half the body color to half more of white/ecru.

Now roll out a little snake of clay – short, stout and pointy (just like Uncle Harold). Echidna spikes are lighter than the body, and they have a dark tip, so brush the tip of the clay point with some darker-colored mica powder (I used PearlEx #661 Antique Copper – but anything brownish will work).

Slice the tip off – about 1cm in length (less than half an inch) will do it.

Next, put a drop of liquid clay on his back (the liquid clay allows the fresh clay to stick on), and press on the clay. Try not to smudge the powder.

Tah dah! A spike. Now do the other five hundred ninety nine thousand, nine hundred ninety nine.

Give him a full bake (check the Polymer Clay Overview in the back for details). Add a patina, if you want to.

Now isn't he precious! Oh, and don't forget, if he goes off to live in the potpourri, add a few more of those little red berries to the mix – he really likes those.

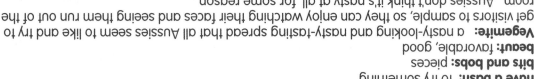

have a bash: to try something

bits and bobs: pieces

beaut: favorable, good

Vegemite: a nasty-looking and nasty-tasting spread that all Aussies seem to like and try to get visitors to sample, so they can enjoy watching their faces and seeing them run out of the room. Aussies don't think it's nasty at all, for some reason.

bonzer: excellent

flash: fancy

dinky-di: genuine

jiggered: worn out

whinge: complain (whinger: whiner, complainer)

chock-a-block: full

galah: foolish person

no worries: don't worry about it, it's all right (this is Australia's unofficial motto, and one reason why Australia is so bonzer!)

bush: forested areas

ripper: really good, outstanding

crikey: oh my good golly gosh!

Oz, the Land Down Under, Aussie - Australia, Australian

g'day : hello, salutations, how are you?

drongo, dag: slow-witted, stupid person

lolly: candy

knackered: tired, physically worn out

rapt: happy, excited

good onya: an statement of approval, as in "you've done well"

POLYMER CLAY OVERVIEW

I just love polymer clay! It is colorful, durable, easy to use. And of course, since it cures at such a low temperature, many embellishments can be added to the clay while you're sculpting. Even more fun!

Always begin by conditioning the clay. Warm up a small amount in your hands by rolling the clay between your palms and twisting. A pasta machine is of course the most useful tool ever invented for polymer clay (and you thought it was for making spaghetti) because it does the work of conditioning and blending for you quickly and thoroughly. Conditioning the clay is crucial to the final durability of the piece, as well as its flexibility while being worked with. As the clay ages, its component ingredients need to be remixed to their "original" state, which is what conditioning does. This also helps prevent cracking when the clay is baked.

Many brands of polymer clay are available, and all are essentially composed of the same basic ingredients. Each brand has its own strengths and quirks. For these projects, **I use and recommend Premo!** brand (made by Sculpey), as a clay especially suited for sculpture. You can use whichever brand is your favorite, and you can mix brands together for any of these projects.

Many tools can be used when working with polymer clay -- wood, metal and plastic are equally functional. Since polymer clay does not thin down with water, you will rely on your tools and your fingers to manipulate, smooth and texture the clay. All tools used for polymer clay should **not** be used with food afterwards.

You can choose to work on any flat, nonporous work surface, such as glass, or marble. Wood can absorb the plasticizers in the clay, staining the wood and hardening your clay, so I recommend sculpting on a piece of thicker cardstock paper. You should not store your clay on card stock, however, as it will absorb plasticizers from the clay, making the clay crumbly. You can store your clay on wax paper or in plastic sandwich bags. It's a good idea to cover your clay, too, when not in use to keep the dust off.

Cleaning your hands when switching colors (so as not to transfer residual color from hands to clay) is important. So is cleanup when you are finished claying. A gritty soap is very helpful in removing the residue. You can also use baby wipes, cold cream, baby oil or rubbing alcohol before soap and water washing.

Baking polymer clay is best accomplished with a home oven or convection oven, although toaster ovens can be adequate when the temperature is supervised, as they have a tendency to overheat (I suspect gremlins). Temperature is critical in the curing of polymer clay. Clay that is cooked at too low a temperature or for too short a time will not adequately cure and can be brittle and easily broken. Always use an oven thermometer and follow the clay manufacturer's instructions. Do not cook at too high a temperature, or clay will burn. Always use adequate ventilation. Do not microwave. Bake in a pan or on a ceramic tile that is designated for clay use only (keep the finished piece on the cardstock before placing it in your cooking pan/tile to prevent the surface touching metal or tile from becoming shiny). If you use a home oven, you should clean the oven before using it again for food baking.

Usually the baking time for sculpture is a minimum of 20 minutes for every quarter inch of thickness at the thickest part of the clay. For most pieces this means a minimum of 30-45 minutes in the oven. I usually bake my pieces for at least 45 minutes, usually an hour.

Cured clay is very durable - so you can pass on your masterpieces as heirlooms to your children and to their children, and their children, and eBay. If you can't finish your project all in one go and want to store it until you can get back to it, take it off the cardstock and place it in a ziploc bag and seal it -- this will keep the dust off until you're ready to play.

DINGO

And that's it! There's lots more to learn about polymer clay - but this is all you need to know to do the projects in this book, and have a successful and fun time while you're at it!

How come I'm not in this book?

supplies: clays, tools and more
There are so many wonderful places to get the supplies for all the projects in this book. Here are **just a few** of my favorites to get you started.

www.ClayFactory.net -- mica powders and clay supplies
www.FireMountainGems.com - beads, findings and tools
www.PolymerClayExpress.com - clay and clay supplies (including varathane)
www.SpecialtyBeads.com -- Italian mesh ribbon, beads

in Australia - here's a few to get you started: www.BeadWithMe.com.au; www.Over the Rainbow.com.au; www.SelonjBeads.com.au; www.creativecraftclass.com

glass eyes - if you liked the glass eyes on the Bunyip (p.38) those eyes are specially made by Ralph McCaskey and you can get them directly from him: www.nightsidestudios.com or from my site: www.CForiginals.com.

Gotta Have It and **Can't Live WithOut It** tools: www.sculpt.com; www.cforiginals.com

information
www.NPCG.org is the National Polymer Clay Guild website. Check it out for polymer guilds, events and classes! It is a wonderful source for keeping up with what's happening in the polymer community (yup, there's a community). The Australian polymer clay artists guild communicates online at: www.polymerclay.com.au/information

www.PolymerClayCentral.com will connect you to every juicy tidbit of information, opinion, and news in the wide, wide world of polymer clay.

www.PolymerClayDaily.com is a polymer clay blog that will probably become your favorite way to start the day.

http://groups.yahoo.com/group/cforiginals is my chat group where the nicest group of polymer enthusiasts swap stories, accomplishments and encouragement. Join us!

www.PolkaDotCreations.com is a wonderful source for books, articles and magazines that have to do with polymer clay.

PolymerCafé magazine is devoted entirely to polymer clay happenings, projects, people. Many other magazines regularly feature polymer articles and projects, too - especially Bead & Button, Step By Step Beads and Bead Unique.

RESOURCES

FINISHING TOUCHES: PATINA AND CLEAR COAT

After your piece is baked and cooled you may want to add a patina to bring out the color and emphasize the details. A patina is an added coloring - in this case, acrylic paint - applied to the finished sculpture. Here's how! 1. paint! any acrylic is great - or mix your color; 2. brush on a small area at a time; 3. immediately wipe off the surface paint using several damp sponges to remove the surface paint, leaving it only in the cracks and texture areas. Clean sponges frequently to avoid a muddy look; 4. All done!

After adding a patina, you may want to coat your piece with a clear, protective coating. All the major brands of clay have some to choose from. Personally, I prefer a very, very low sheen - organic sculptures are better with satin or matte finishes, or no finishes at all. I use Rustoleum's Varathane (Diamond Water-based polyurethane -- style #200241, 200261). It's an outdoor varnish that just happens to be wonderful on polymer clay!!

Brush the clear coating on after the clay is baked and the patina is dry. Do not coat over any beads or other embellishments you may have used.

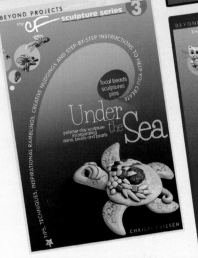